BEYOND EXPECTATIONS

poems by

Cada McCoy

Finishing Line Press
Georgetown, Kentucky

BEYOND EXPECTATIONS

ACKNOWLEDGMENTS

With special thanks to Upstate Poets, Greenville, SC; Furman University's
Osher Lifelong Learning Institute; and, above all, Arthur McMaster—poet,
instructor, and inspirer extraordinaire.

Publisher: Leah Huete de Maines
Editor: Christen Kincaid
Cover Art: Arcada Robinson Fleming, Rehoboth Beach, DE, 1910
Author Photo: Eric Schweitzer
Cover Design: Robin McCoy, robinmccoy.com

Order online: www.finishinglinepress.com
also available on amazon.com

Author inquiries and mail orders:
Finishing Line Press
PO Box 1626
Georgetown, Kentucky 40324
USA

Contents

At times our own light goes out and is rekindled by a spark from another person. Each of us has cause to think with deep gratitude of those who have lighted the flame within us.
—Albert Schweitzer

Beyond Expectations

At thirty, before the War in Eastern Shore Society,
she was rued a spinster, so when sacramental vows
were at last exchanged in the papist parish hall
dwarfed by Mother of All Sorrows
and announced in The Sunday Times,
even the Presbyterian ladies fanned themselves,
relieved,

seeing her hope chest swell with allusions to
lace curtains, illusions of oak alleyways.
And pride. The embossed Crane & Co.
linen monogrammed acknowledgments held
hints of magnolia, so when gently knifed open,
even the Presbyterian ladies, in righteous self-delusion,
believed.

Save for at forty, beaten, she stoically surrendered
finespun, no match for shanty panes and tarnished
Reed & Barton and moth-holed Harris Tweed
when vanquished hope imprisoned empty pride.
Even the Presbyterian ladies denied what she could have
conceived.

Still she did. And the daughter born on that
sacrificial battleground unraveled
petite point samplers to cast on a real trousseau,
mail unchained from dynastical fairy tales,
filled the chest anew, wise now that
even the Presbyterian ladies could not sway
truth-armed women who refuse to be
deceived.

Othering

For Wilhelminia Sweeper Warner, 1913-1978

Bound to make us other, better folk,
each day our other mothers came
from the other side of truth, broke
from where other games are played.

Each day our other mothers came
from along the other side of tracks
from where other games are played
with rules begat from skittish facts.

From along the other side of tracks,
somewhere beyond the other school,
with rules begat from skittish facts
of waiting rooms and swimming pools,

somewhere beyond the other school
where history warns the others' own
of waiting rooms and swimming pools,
our other mothers set out from home.

Where history warns the others' own
across town and another world away,
our other mothers set out from home,
alone, to just get by for one more day.

Across town and half a world away,
our other mothers leave their own
alone to just get by for one more day,
bound to make us other, better folk.

What Would People Think

about us, our place
in this narrow town, my mother
fretted, her face to my face,
four years unsullied,
between iron palms
that bruised, warned
I should never, would never,
tell of the stranger who
hushed my lips as Hi-Ho silvered
away in Saturday matinee dark.
Then
when ten times the time had passed,
my blind dog lay on the cool steel's span
—such a slight reach, really—
for this town's hallowed healer
of all small and innocent things who
startled my face to his face
between iron palms,
his lips bruised, warned
I should never, would never,
tell because I knew too well
what people, what you, would think.

Catholic Criming

How could a tender child of seven years,
know what sin is, let alone confess?
Yet, contrition's key to stepping forth
holy in flowered veil and frilly dress.

In Saturday's sorry twilight queue
on St. John's stained-glass path, I stall.
My hallelujah rests just out of reach,
enshrined with Father Mike (who's heard it all).

An idea dawns: I'll invent my sin—
How about greed? Or, even better, pride?
Envy? Something worse? Wait! Will my penance
for that sin wipe its underlying lie?

As the wicked onward wind, I frizzle
as dawns the miraculous solution:
Just confess my "sin," then *quick* tack on "fib"
to score umbrella absolution!

When I kneel in the penitent's booth,
I hear better angels commence to pray
for one more confessional professional
ready for her First Communion Day.

Catholic Criming: Another Point of View

Here they come again, he thinks, dodging
into the booth, slipping the Altar Guild
committee milling in the vestibule
like some deranged florists, God forbid!

Another Saturday, and Father Mike's
stew's bubbling back on the rectory's range,
the blessed Bordeaux, uncorked, is breathing,
beckoning, setting deep desires aflame.

He settles in proprietarily,
to stroke the stole soft about his neck,
lift his hand to the one dot of light that
sets off his gold ring to its best effect.

Afflicted parishioners interrupt
his dreams of the bishop's coming visit
when surely he'll be granted his coveted
parish-to-cathedral upgrade ticket.

Another penitent wrenches aside
the heavy drapes of the confessional.
A child kneels down, her curly head below
his gaze that's grown impatient, cynical.

Something like the sound of fluttering wings
obsures the first words of her confession,
then "fib" emerges, and he yawns, bored with
these small humans' trivial transgressions.

"Pray five *Our Fathers* and ten *Hail Marys*,"
Father Mike intones. "Oh, and, sin no more,"
he adds, knowing that she will, providing
job security for his clergy corps.

When the last sinner has confessed, atoned,
and most assured of the Divine's design,
the priest humbly folds his soft hands convinced,
"To err is human; forgiveness is but mine."

Mondegreenery

Miss O'Keefe tap-taps, tap-taps, tap-taps
in metronomic monotony,
squints at the dozen ten-year-olds
shuffling on her dusty riser steps.
Sing!
Miss O'Keefe demands and strangles
America from the upright's jaundiced keys.
Stop!
Miss O'Keefe commands and stabs
the pencil behind her ear. A glare, knobby finger
pressed to wrinkled lips. Silenced forever
one small innocent's song. One song.
Earworms starve, twist in fallow, salted ground
while tone-deaf dissonance roots in deep.
Lyrical nonsense makes the only sense where
sweet dreams are made of cheese,
dancing queens feel beats from tangerines,
and The Beatles want to hold my ham.
Doomed to confused tunelessness, I often imagine
Miss O'Keefe had never looked my way.

Runs & Refrains

Remembering a maple-freckled sapling swaying on hardwood,
eyes steady on threads of some greater goal while at his knees
swirled native old-growth green and gold sprung from
low country loam. Of a cultivar named for fortune, he was
a late transplant, an exotic variety, our invasive curiosity.

Remembering he grew large on a court of bigger stage,
frailing and fretting Saturday night Seeger songs
of rambling land, passing flowers and Alby Jay,
bartering notes on good old America's folk stories
embellished for his own underground passage.

Remembering pocketed paper crushed against my cheek
on a lyceum evening of sweet grass and stirrings.
"Come with us," he said. "It's not too late."
But it was too late or, perhaps, too early to reckon that
sometimes storms blow too hard, bending is no choice when
history recalls, repeats its chorus of terminal refrains.

Remembering now and finding him firm rooted, weathered tall
on his rocky ridge, freckles faded memories under aging snows.
I click my fingers, and his yesterday's voice fills half a century
rising above province hemlocks in a northern morning mist.

This time, would I say yes?

Getting Ready for Bed with Robin, aged four

Upon reading "Listening to Peter and the Wolf with Jason, aged three" by A.E. Stallings

Shadows long, pj's on, prayers said,
he crawls onto his trundle bed,
snuggles down for the nightly drill ahead.

From among his most favored toys,
he's picked Batman, Spidey, two GI Joes,
brave action figures made for little boys

who insist on evening armaments
against ghosts, ghouls, bogeymen, and hints
of monsters trailing phantom footprints

behind his closet door and curtains drawn
tight against the wind that whispers, spawns
creatures who always vanish with the dawn.

Slowly, deliberately, I scrutinize
his room, then demonstrate I've exorcised
every scary demon he's imaginized,

make a spectacle of spirit-shooing
in all the spaces where any spooking
might originate; but alarmed, he's pointing

to the sliver-slit between his bed and floor.
I sigh, lean down, slow count to ten before
launching my de-witching pitch of last resort:

"Not one thing could fit between, understand?
Not. One. Hair. Not the tiniest grain of sand."
"Oh, Mommy," he breathes, eyes wide. "*Flatman* can."

Hatch

For Robin

*Gone out to see many great and
wondrous things.*
Etched in fledgling artist's hand, pristine words,
a bright chit on the pantry door amidst debris
from ebb of what we did, flow of yet to do.
This paper prophesy sticks crisp and square,
yolk golden as the car's ghost
that shimmers new outside our door.
Big Bird we'd laughed and christened it,
feeding the restless flutters in our nest.

Days, decades dulled to bistre tones,
and just before the movers come,
I peel away the eggshell promise signed
Your Child
—our compact long since satisfied.

A Case for Mr. Darwin's Textbook

This spring, it's the ladder
the wren chooses
precarious against the tool shed,
while her cocky cousins,
remnants of decimated generations,
fluff off shadows of fern baskets
toppled by every storm,
post box open to deadly deliveries,
crushing crevasses in patio chairs.

So, no surprise the ginger cat perches,
twitching, on edge above while
a quick sliver of snake measures up the rungs.
We watched and knew.
We couldn't watch because we knew.

Today, we happened by the window and saw
three soft balls tumble from their ledge, wings lift,
genes fat from undying nest-fail fare, eyeing
next spring and the sconces by the door.

Bound

Our dogs have always loved
a good scratch about the neck,
old collars slipped off. I suspect
our dogs have always loved

a good scratch about the neck,
a moment freed from our constraints,
unleashed, lolling, no complaints.
A good scratch about the neck,

a moment freed from our constraints,
which left her, alone, eyes terror wide,
to pant, whine, lean hard against my side.
A moment freed from our constraints

which left her, alone, eyes terror wide,
recalling collars just donned for show
for all who came, then went, long ago,
which left her alone, eyes terror wide.

Recalling collars just donned for show,
we kept her leather band in place,
for a lifetime buckled snug erased
recalling collars just donned for show.

We kept her leather band in place,
until it came time for her to pass
to where all good dogs go. At the last,
we kept her leather band in place.

Our dogs have always loved
a good scratch about the neck,
old collars slipped off. I suspect
our dogs have always loved.

Hey, Neighbor, There's an App for That!

"What's on your mind, neighbor?" It sure seems friendly
clicking on Nextdoor's conversational stream
of sales, services, volunteer assemblies,
and someone's lost pet (the ever-constant theme).

Clicking on Nextdoor's conversational stream,
feral cats, mailbox theft, porch pirates, gun shots
and someone's lost pet (the ever-constant theme)
are stirring real anxiety on *our* block.

Feral cats, mailbox theft, porch pirates, gun shots.
Not bad enough? Now, those kids up to no good
are stirring real anxiety on our block,
video-captured on the lawn where they stood!

Not bad enough? Now, those kids up to no good,
making the effort to return a lost pet,
video-captured on the lawn where they stood.
Won't somebody just give these children credit?

Making the effort to return a lost pet
now drowned in neighbors' fear-mongering frenzy.
Won't somebody just give these children credit
before this get-off-my-lawn town turns deadly?

Now drowned in neighbors' fear-mongering frenzy,
no posts of good kids and saved pets are trending
before this get-off-my-lawn town turns deadly.
"What's on your mind, neighbor?" It sure seems friendly.

It's Curtains

An innocent enough request
from the overseer of the
community's gathering place
for willing workers to buff and fluff
the dreary hall burdened with its weakened,
worn trappings of times past since
no spring...or fall or winter, for that matter...
sprucing when plague had sent these dwellers
underground
to at last emerge into dust-muted rays.
It's time, they said, then gathered nerve,
and took the cue to do
something.
They never blinked, but reached, uplifted.
Warmth streamed, horizons brightened.

When word spread throughout the village
of the new enlightenment, enraged others
rushed to scour obsessive garages
for pitchforks, torches, and blame.

"Comedy or tragedy?" The audience whispers
restless in their seats as the curtains come down.

What's Playing in the Retirement Village?

How can it be that we, yesterday young,
now find ourselves in this threadbare lobby,
trembling tickets held tight, waiting among
the tiredly resigned to this shoddy
re-run of days, weeks, years, merely copied,
colorized to hold fast our attention
while sharp scenes dissolve and rising tension
drains from ancient reels that wobble, teeter,
and stubbornly replay this dated run,
life's final low budget second feature.

Street Gang

One by one, they gather on the corner,
each one slipping in beside the other,
sporting teals and mauves, and on their feet
the latest styles of walking shoes compete
to kick off the day's chatty competition
of recipes focused on the best nutrition
needed to revive declining cognition.

Sometimes four, maybe six, depending
on the weather (and other muted matters)
strike out pretending sleepless nights
or failing knees aren't slowing
their pace as they wheel around the flowing
streets of the 'hood, voices shrill with laughter,
keeping all talk of personal disaster
*sotto voc*e in their streams of constant chatter.

Wide brims tugged snug over spot tattoos
sunshine-etched when carefree days of youth
held no fear—could not imagine—such a time
when even bookish nerds and beauty queens
would be leveraged together by life's stolen goods.

It's Telling

"How did you two meet?"
The question struggles through dining room decibels,
starched server hovering, pencil floating,
and the man replies,
"Well, during that blizzard of '72…"
"Oh, no," his wife chides, "Remember, honey,
it wasn't snowing…"
"You tell the story, dear." He, accustomed, bows out
while she does, and their server attends those
waiting to toast this half-century mark,
leaning forward now to hear about
"The wedding?"
He lifts his glass, swirls the aged Bordeaux.
"It was raining," he starts, but she laughs, gives her head a shake.
"Don't you recall how the sun broke through that morning?"
He acquiesces to her, their history;
then, the server reveals the cake—surprising her—
and its showers of glitter, golden flakes bring a gasp,
her hand laid on his, applause from their small gathering.
"Oh, sweetie!" She gazes into his eyes.
"You never tell me anything."

Acer Rubrum

She twirls the glass that holds her wine,
and marking time,
awaits the shift
of season's drift.

With one last sip from summer's cup,
she now holds up
her chalice for
the fine red pour.

Bordeaux overflows, her glass tips
to sprinkle chips
of garnet gems
on autumn's hems.

Abscission

Summer sighs, spent,
and I sense her breath
sharp in autumn's drift,
harlequin threads released
in one sudden windless storm
to rattle, rain, dance, tumble, sway,
these rustling cascades of spangles
in morning's mint-frosted light,
these bright ballerinas and toy tops spinning,
spiraling, twirling past burnished oak cradles
slipping gently from side-to-side drifting
as one long breathless whisper
            down
                    down
                            down
to be snared mid-air, they say, brings luck,
so, reach out, stretch up to feel
this old forest's shed blessings
ablaze anew in the palm of your hand.

**Do Not
Think of a
Polar Bear!**
As you meander
through the following lines,
with just enough attention and just enough time, can you unstick the
picture stuck in your mind? Immediately deny any images related to
Ursus maritimus: a snowy pelt, coal black nose, teddy on an icy floe.
How are you doing? Is it working as you try to fully blot
out that one devilish, bearish, stalking thought? It's this
twisted brain legerdemain that hucksters and politicos
exploit because you cannot deny an idea unless
you first deploy it, cannot unimagine a bear
unless you first imagine one. And, once a
shape substantiates, it cannot be undone.
Now, here at last,   I can only wonder
what's roaming in   your head's tundra.
Wouldn't be a white   polar bear, would it?

*Musings on Fyodor Dostoevsky's "Winter Notes on Summer Impressions"; Daniel
Wegner's Ironic Process Theory ("the white bear problem"); and Lewis Carroll's shape
poem, "The Mouse's Tale."*

Coming Up Right After the Weather

The feed was all a-Twitter with photos
of squatter Arctic bears camped in stations
emptied of forecasters who once showed us
reassuring clips of stable glaciers,
deep sea ice, immeasurable snow cover.
But today's grisly prognostications
are left to those roiled from their winter snooze
when their home's alarm sounded way too soon.

Exotic Animal Amnesty Day

happened to fall on the Saturday
their Gators faced those Seminoles,
but his dad reassured him a pickup
trip down to the Everglades would be
as good, better even, seeing how
his sinewy pet would thrive on
the state's free native buffet.

Barking Mad Exotic Encounter's owner
had encouraged their purchase, said
it bought freedom, for God's sake, from
Big Brother overreach into
small business commerce when, you know,
what planetary harm could possibly come
from one little boy owning one little snake.

When a distant, warm September Saturday
trapped them soggily atop the pool table with
failing cell phones held dispairingly aloft,
they looked down to see the magnificent python
rippling, rising, falling, undulating along
the hurricane's tidal surge, dead set on
the state's free native buffet.

A Chance, Perchance?

Mother sighs,
shakes her shawl and scrapes her shoes,
swirls her skirts of storm-tossed sky.

Faith frizzled,
she'd pitched pestilence amidst
tempest's squalls and flame's sizzle.

Mother smiles.
Fortune favors lessons learned.
Come to a conclusion, child?

Betrayed by His Diet Coke Valet

Distraught calls went out from Justice to three
sharp-razored sages when subpoenas proved
inadequate to solve the mystery
of boxes that appeared to have been moved.

Messrs. Occam, Hitchens, and Hanlon, hence
engaged, told the Feebies: keep it simple;
unearth unimpeachable evidence;
assume stupidity, not a swindle.

Agents followed the philosophers' leads,
spied a security camera that
nailed the president's man doing the deed
which is what leveraged him into a rat.

Shame Agatha wasn't first conferred with
'cause she would have known the butler did it.

Book Ban Efforts Spread Across the U.S.

The New York Times, Jan. 30, 2022
Parents, activists, school board officials and lawmakers around
the country are challenging books at a pace not seen in decades.

By half past ten, the meeting had lasted way too long, they agreed,
although the council members were stuck at item three
on the agenda, what with all the people stomping, waving signs,
chanting. (Reports of unlicensed carry were later denied.)

While security cleared the room, a motion seconded, passed
judgment on *all* the inflammatory books, majority steadfast
though they'd only worked down to Silverstein on the list.
(Mere expediency, not appeasement, Live Five at 11 insisted.)

And, that was how *Where the Sidewalk Ends* vanished altogether
from the stacks at the county library, but, just for good measure,
at their next monthly meeting, council slashed the library's funding.
When AP ran the story, *Money* magazine sent headquarters-hunting

corporations elsewhere to live. Owners of the market franchise,
by now you've probably heard, reorganized, then downsized,
finally shuttered the town's last lingering grocery store.
These days, few attend municipal meetings with little more

on belt-tightened dockets but cuts to the walkability program
since the police chief's adamant demand for more cops to scram
those homeless camped at the ghosted Piggly Wiggly and run
calls on kids trespassing beyond the beat-up boards that warn:

SIDEWALK ENDS

Sounds Good, Freedom Does

"Look," they said. Heads nodded,
smug fingers crooked toward the brook
trickling, tinkling, clearly raw and free
of municipal disinfection dumps,
fluoride, pharmaceuticals,
heavy metals, mind-controlling drugs.
Brimming with all the benefits of
nature's healing, they were told,
compounded with rare natural minerals,
sold for a low, low price and free delivery.
Thinking back, no one could recall
the surcharge for spores that teemed
amongst the sodden, rotting twigs
where those wakes of vultures
freely disgorged their bilge
above the sparkling headstream.

In a Deep Red State of Mind

First line from "Learning to be a Panda"-Sonya Larson; Kenyon Review, Jan/Feb 2021

It's as if everyone is a little pregnant right now,
staying our breaths, cloaking our essence
braced for what's coming, and how
it's as if everyone is

tentatively touching each tumescence
of abominable seed planted, plowed
deep, leaving no just way to excise sins

conceived by righteous holier-than-thou
manned midwifery obsessed with
ensuring we're all expectantly cowed.
It's as if everyone is.

Crux of the Matter

At cobbled crossroads near about anywhere,
a jangle and crank of a wagon appears
swaddled in incense that sulphers the air.
Pall lifts. A woman standing there?
Why, she could be my Mother!

Cheap Thrills, Bargains Galore,
Easy Answers To All Your Woes
snaps the brassy banner
with heaving hooks of
cassocks, rings, collars, yellowed ruffs,
gilt sashes and wreathes,
crowns and skeletons, pyrite saucers of oil,
a buffalo's head on a pike.
Delusions and miracles,
garments fundamental all at half price.
Along with a few jaundiced books.

So, what are you selling today?
Whatever you're buying, she says with a wink.
Whichever way the ill wind's blowing,
the most you're willing to pay.

Calming potions cut with simple solutions
and elixirs magic to bolster belief.
Emetics of antimony, two for the price of one.
A packet of sins to wheedle forgiveness,
holy ablutions, transmogrified dilutions,
if the offer is right.
A few incantations for the cost of a song,
rusty remnants and relics, votives, a straw cross,
mummified babies, tarnished burial masks.
A sheaf of splinters, nectars, a cap,
and a good god's laugh—
the real deal of the day.

Faith rattles from her Pandora's box,
Jack in the pulpit squats on his shelf.
She fingers the top of a pottery jar:
Here's Fear and Hate bottled up real tight
(always works better if taken at night.)

Can't tempt you with nothing? She shrugs. Suspect
you'll be back for discounted resurrected regrets.

Willow whip in hand, the coachman makes
a hard right turn.
Surely, there's someone out there
in need of a snake.

How do we know when to let go of our end of the rope?

Born, raised and having returned for decades to South Carolina's Lowcountry, **Cada McCoy** went north to retire in the shadow of the Blue Ridge mountains after a string of careers littered with words—librarian, corporate publications editor, independent bookstore owner. Now, she writes and occasionally instructs in Furman University's OSHER Lifelong Learning Institute, offering limited editing services to her fellow scribes. One of the first women students when Clemson transitioned from an agricultural/military college to a university, there she earned her undergraduate degree in English and, later, received an MA from Webster University. While also pursuing her passion for textile art, Cada resides in Greenville with her architect husband, Pembroke Welsh corgi, and thesaurus.

www.ingramcontent.com/pod-product-compliance
Lightning Source LLC
Chambersburg PA
CBHW022051080426
42734CB00009B/1293